Weather

FRED MARTIN

Heinemann

First published in Great Britain by Heinemann Library
Halley Court, Jordan Hill, Oxford OX2 8EJ
a division of Reed Educational & Professional Publishing Ltd

MELBOURNE AUCKLAND
FLORENCE PRAGUE MADRID ATHENS
SINGAPORE TOKYO CHICAGO SAO PAULO
PORTSMOUTH NH MEXICO
IBADAN GABORONE JOHANNESBURG
KAMPALA NAIROBI

Designed by Artistix
Illustrations by Scorpio Design & Illustration
Originated by Dot Gradations Ltd.
Printed in Hong Kong

00 99
10 9 8 7 6 5 4 3

284923

JSS1·5

ISBN 0 431 06434 2
This title is also available in a hardback library edition (ISBN 0 431 06439 3)

British Library Cataloguing in Publication Data

Martin, Fred, 1948 –
    Weather. – (Themes in geography)
    1. Weather – Juvenile literature
    I. Title II. Series
    551.6

Acknowledgements
The Publishers would like to thank the following for permission to reproduce photographs.
Ace Photo Agency/Journalism Services: p.35, Ace Photo Agency/Paul Thompson: p.40, Barnaby's Picture Library: p.21, Barnaby's Picture Library/Alan R Smith: p.20, Bruce Coleman/Alantide SDF: p.24, Cephas Picture Library/Andrew Kelly: p.36, Crown copyright. Reproduced with the permission of the Controller of Her Majesty's Stationery Office: p.22, p.23, Frank Spooner Pictures/Gamma: p.26, Fred Martin: p.9, p.14, p.15, p.37, p.38, GSF Picture: p.7, J Allan Cash: p.10, p.31, Magnum/Rene Burri: p.16, Panos Pictures/Jeremy Hartley: p.6, p.28, Robert Harding Picture Library/Gavin Hellier: p.11, Science Photo Library/European Space Agency: p.19, Still Pictures/Andre Bartschi: p.42, Still Pictures/Helour Netocny: p.43, Still Pictures/Jorgen Schytte: p.39, Still Pictures/Mark Edwards: p.5, p.8, p.44, Still Pictures/Paul Harrison: p.42, The Environmental Picture Library/ Irene R Langui: p.13, The Image Bank/AT Willett: p.30, The Image Bank/Bill Varie: p.29, The Image Bank/David Hamilton: p.25, The Image Bank/Eric Meola: p.34, The Image Bank/John Kelly: p.4, The Image Bank/Robert Holland: p.27, The Image Bank/Stephen Wilkes: p.12, The Image Bank/Ted Russell: p.33, Tony Stone Images/James Balog: p.33, Tony Stone Images/Jane Gifford: p.41

Cover photograph reproduced with permission of Tony Stone Images.

Our thanks to Clare Boast, Sutherland Primary School, Stoke on Trent, for her comments in the preparation of this book.

Every effort has been made to contact copyright holders of any material reproduced in this book. Any omissions will be rectified in subsequent printings if notice is given to the Publisher.

Contents

Have a nice day

People often talk about the weather. This is because it affects so many things that we do. The food we eat depends on the weather. Many of the sports we play depend on the weather. Even what we wear depends on what the weather is like.

Always changing

A weather **forecast** describes how conditions change. Sometimes the weather changes very quickly. Clear sunny skies in the morning can change to rain in the afternoon. One reason for this is because the Earth heats up by different amounts during the day. The amount of heat affects the clouds, the wind and every other part of the weather.

The weather also changes from day to day. A day of rain can be replaced by sunshine and showers. In the UK, a spell of settled weather is less common than changeable weather.

A wet day in the mountains of California, USA.

Heavy rain has already flooded the road.

The cyclist has dressed to stay dry and warm.

People enjoying the sun at Rimini in Italy.

There is a clear blue sky and sunshine.

There is a breeze from the sea but the air temperature is about 35°C.

What makes weather?

The air changes in many ways to give different types of weather. The **temperature** is how hot or cold it is. This is easy to feel and to measure. A figure for the amount of heat is given in degrees of centigrade or Fahrenheit. The instrument used to measure temperature is called a **thermometer**.

Clouds can be seen and their effects can be felt. Clouds are a sign that there is water in the air. It may comes down as rain or snow, or stay in the air as humidity.

The wind shows that air is moving from one place to another. This can bring warm or cold temperatures from one place to another. It can also blow water from the oceans to form clouds and fall as rain over the land.

The weather machine

The weather is like a giant machine made from many different parts. A change to one part has an effect on all the other parts. Cooling changes **water vapour** into clouds. Clouds block out the sun and make the temperature colder. Differences in heat also make the winds blow. No wonder the weather forecasters find it so hard to be accurate all the time!

Did you know?

The sun is a burning ball of gas. It is about 93 million miles from the Earth.

The Earth is surrounded by a layer of air. There is no air in open space beyond this layer.

Light and heat from the sun take 8 minutes to travel to the Earth.

Heating the Earth

The Earth is about 93 million miles from the sun. It would be too hot to live on the Earth if the sun was much nearer. It would be too cold if it was much further.

Sunlight and heat

The sun's energy comes to the Earth as **radiation**. This is what gives us both light and heat. The sun's radiation passes through a layer of gases around the Earth called the **atmosphere**.

The atmosphere is about 800 km thick. Most of the gases are found nearest the Earth in a layer called the **troposphere**. The air is said to be 'thin' where there are fewer gases higher up. The sun's heat beams down through the atmosphere until it reaches the ground.

Warmed from below

Low-lying land is warmed the most by the sun. This is because the air is more dense lower down. This denser air absorbs more heat than the thinner air higher up. This is why it is colder by 6.5°C for every 1000 metres of height.

Some of the sun's heat is reflected back into space by the clouds before it reaches the ground. Heat rising back from the ground warms the air above it.

The Alps mountain range in France.

The highest mountain peaks are always so cold that snow and ice do not completely melt.

Winter in the UK at 2.30PM.

The sun is very low in the sky.

The low angle means the light and heat are spread out over a large area so the temperature stays low.

Sun at an angle

Some places on Earth are much hotter than others. One reason for this is because of the angle of the sun's rays as they reach the ground. The Earth absorbs more heat when the sun is high in the sky than when the sun's angle is low. When the sun is low, the heat is spread over a much larger area than when it is high.

The curve of the Earth means that the sun never shines at a high angle on places near the North and the South Poles. These places can never get warm. Over the equator, the sun does shine at a high angle so it can get very much hotter.

During the day, the sun reaches its highest angle at midday. It is much lower in the sky in the early morning and later in the evening. This explains why it is warmer at midday than in the early morning or late evening.

Land and sea

The sun warms the land more than the seas and oceans. Light and heat go much deeper into the seas so they do not warm up as much.

But the land loses heat much faster and becomes much colder than the seas. This is why places nearest the oceans have a small difference during the year between the hottest and coldest temperatures. Places further from an ocean with the same sun's angle have a greater temperature range.

Did you know?

The highest angle the sun ever reaches at the North and South Poles is only $23\frac{1}{2}$ degrees. For 6 months, the sun does not rise above the horizon at all.

Hot and cold

A valley in Germany with steep slopes.

The south-facing slope is used for growing grapes and other crops.

The colder, north-facing slope is used for growing trees.

Have you noticed how it can be warm in one place, but much cooler only a few metres away? This is because of the ways that the ground can be different.

Aspect and temperature

The warmest places are on slopes that face the sun. These face the south in most parts of the northern half of the Earth.

The direction a slope faces is called its **aspect**. The ground becomes warmer because the slope tilts the land to make a higher angle with the sun's rays. On a north-facing slope, the sun's rays are slanted away at a shallow angle so it is much cooler.

Some crops need more heat than others. Farmers have to choose the best slope for each crop.

Reflecting heat

The colour of the ground also affects the **temperature**. Pale colours reflect the light back again so the heat does not warm the ground.

In cold areas such as Antarctica, the snow and ice reflect back most of the sun's heat. Places with darker colours such as forests and dark rocks take in more heat.

In the shade

The best way to get out of the heat is to find some shade. Very little light gets through the tree tops of a dense forest. On the ground, the temperature is much cooler. Only shade-loving plants such as lichens and mosses can grow there.

A misty morning

At night, cold air from the mountains can drain down into a valley. This is because cold air is heavier than warm air. The warmer and more humid air in the valley becomes colder. Water in the air changes to tiny water droplets that make the air become misty.

When the sun rises, the valley can be full of mist. The sun heats up the land above the valley but it takes longer for it to burn away the mist. The mist stops heat from reaching the valley bottom. This makes a **temperature inversion**, where, for a while, the air in the valley bottom is colder than the air over higher land above it.

Did you know?

In a tropical rain forest, only about 2% of the sunlight is able to get to the forest floor.

Shade in a tropical rain forest in Brazil.

Tall trees with wide, dense leaves block out most of the sunlight.

9

Windy weather

You can see and feel the air when it moves. Clouds travel across the sky, leaves blow about and you can even feel it on your face. The movement of air is called wind.

Wind movements

Winds blow in wide bands across the Earth. In some places, the wind blows from one direction for most of the year. These are called **prevailing winds**.

Winds blow warm air to places that are cold. They also blow cold air to places that are warm. Cold air blows from the North and South Poles.

Warm air rises and spreads north and south from the equator. **Trade winds** move air back to the equator.

British westerlies

The prevailing wind over the British Isles is from the southwest. The Atlantic Ocean lies to the southwest. This helps create weather that is mostly wet and mild.

In the UK, the coldest days are in winter when the wind blows from the north or the east. These winds come from the icy Arctic Ocean and the cold interior of Asia.

A windy hillside in County Down, Northern Ireland.

The tree branches have been blown to one side.

The wind blows mainly from the southwest over the UK.

Monsoon winds

In some places, the wind blows from different directions at different times of the year. This is what happens over India and other countries in South-East Asia.

This type of climate is called a **monsoon**. A change in the wind direction brings very different **temperatures** and rainfall.

Between October and March, a dry wind blows from the north out of central Asia. The rainfall at Bombay in India for these months is less than 10 cm each month. For the rest of the year, warm, wet air blows from the south across the Indian Ocean. This brings rainfall of up to 60 cm in July.

The Beaufort scale

The strength of the wind is measured on the **Beaufort scale**. This scale labels the wind strength from Force 1 to Force 12.

At Force 1, the wind blows at up to 5 kph. This is known as 'light air'. By Force 8, there is a **gale** blowing at between 62 and 74 kph. This is enough to break branches from trees and it becomes hard to walk without being blown over. At Force 12, there is a **hurricane** with wind speeds at over 120 kph.

A ship battles through a Force 12 hurricane.

*The **shipping forecast** tells the ship's captain how strong the wind will be on the Beaufort scale.*

Did you know?

Some of the strongest winds are high up in a band of the *atmosphere* called the jet stream. The wind speed is up to 500 kph.

Air moves from places where the air pressure is high to where it is low. This is what happens when air is released from a balloon. The air rushes out from the high-pressure area inside to where the air pressure is lower outside.

The seasons

Most people have a favourite time of the year as far as weather is concerned. A part of the year with its own type of weather is called a season.

Four seasons

There are four seasons in some places such as in the UK. The seasons are known as winter, spring, summer and autumn. Each season has a different average **temperature** and amount of rain.

There is not usually a sudden change from one season to the other. Changes in the seasons are shown by changes in plant growth and how different animals behave. People also change what they do depending on the season.

Tropical seasons

Other places have seasonal changes that are very different. In parts of Africa, there are places where it is hot all year with very little rain for 6 months. During the other 6 months, rain sometimes falls during thunderstorms. Words such as winter and summer do not mean much in these places.

Along the equator, there is very little difference in temperature and rainfall from day to day, all year round. This means there are no seasons. Plants grow at the same rate all year round.

A scene in northeastern USA during the autumn.

The weather is becoming too cold for the leaves to go on growing.

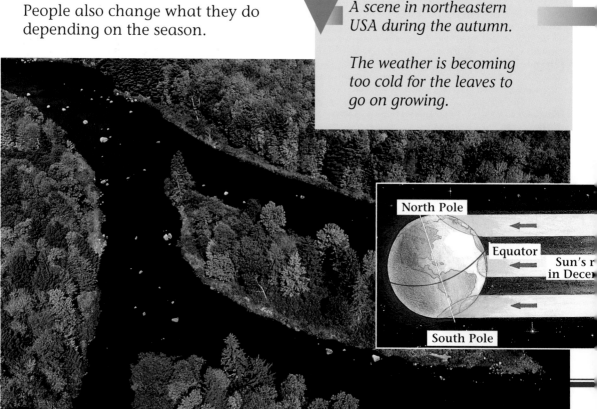

North Pole

Equator

Sun's r
in Dece

South Pole

Labels on diagram: North Pole, Sun's rays in June, Equator, South Pole

The dry season in northern Nigeria near to the Sahara desert.

*In the **savannah climate** of Africa, the coldest season has a temperature of 25°C. The hottest season has a temperature of 35°C.*

The reasons for seasons

Seasons are caused by the Earth moving around the sun. The Earth is always tilted at an angle to the sun. For half the year, the northern half is tilted towards the sun. The angle of the sun is much higher in the sky so the heat is greatest. A half of the Earth is called a **hemisphere**. The sun is highest in the sky over the northern hemisphere on June 22nd. This day is called the **summer solstice**. It has the longest period of daylight in 24 hours of any day of the year. It is sometimes called 'the longest day'.

By December 22nd, the northern hemisphere is tilted away from the sun so it is lower in the sky. This day is called the winter solstice. The period of daylight in 24 hours is the shortest on this day, sometimes called 'the shortest day'. On March 22nd and September 22nd, there is an equal period of day and night in the 24 hours. These days are called the Spring and Autumn **equinoxes**.

Seasons down under

In the southern hemisphere, all the seasons are at opposite times to those in the north. This is because the sun's angle is higher in the sky at the exact opposite time of the year.

Did you know?

Plants do not usually grow when the average temperature in a month is below 6°C.

Places between the Tropic of Cancer and the Tropic of Capricorn have two times of the year when the temperature is hottest. This is because the sun passes directly overhead twice.

The Earth is tilted at an angle of $66\frac{1}{2}$ degrees as it moves around the sun.

Types of clouds

High level streaks of cloud are called cirrus.

The long streak is made by fast winds at high altitude.

Cloud shape depends on how it has been formed, the time of day and the height of the cloud. The sky alters as clouds change their shape. Clouds give useful clues about the weather.

Forms of water

Water exists in the air in different forms. It can be a liquid that falls as rain. Water can also be a gas called **water vapour** that cannot be seen. When water is frozen, it becomes a solid called ice. This happens when the temperature falls below 0°C.

Water changes from a liquid to a gas when the air becomes warmer.

Heat **evaporates** the water and changes it to water vapour. This is why wet clothes hung out in the sun soon become dry again as the water evaporates.

If the temperature cools down again, the water vapour changes back to a liquid. This is called **condensation**.

Billions of droplets

Clouds form when rising water vapour cools down. The water vapour changes to tiny droplets of water. Clouds are made from billions of these condensed droplets of water. It can rain if the droplets become too big and heavy to stay in the sky.

Cumulus and stratus

There are three different names given to clouds based on how they look. A fluffy cloud on its own is called a **cumulus** cloud. The sides and top are white but the underneath can be grey. Clouds in layers are called **stratus** clouds. Very high streaks of cloud are called **cirrus** clouds.

Up in the clouds

Clouds form at different levels in the atmosphere. There are alto-stratus and alto-cumulus clouds at between 3000 and 8000 metres high. The highest clouds found at heights of up to 12,000 metres are the cirro-cumulus and cirro-stratus clouds.

Cumulus cloud at low level.

Air rises when the ground is heated.

Rising moist air cools down and tiny water droplets are formed.

Odd names

Some types of clouds have names that remind people of their shape. The top of a cumulus cloud can spread out at the top to look like a tomahawk or an anvil.

A 'mackerel sky' is when high level cumulus cloud looks like the scales of a mackerel. Long curved cirrus clouds look like 'mares' tails'. These are caused by very fast winds high up in the atmosphere.

Did you know?

There are about 100 different names for types of clouds.

A high-flying jet aircraft leaves a contrail in the sky. A contrail is caused by vapour from the engine fuel that suddenly condenses in the cold air.

Sunshine and showers

A glider stays in the air helped by rising currents of warm air called thermals.

Rising air cools to form cumulus clouds.

Rain from a cumulus cloud is called convection rain.

It is useful to be able to **forecast** when it will rain. This is done by studying the type of clouds, the **temperature**, air pressure and how much moisture is in the air. Also, there is more chance of rain in some places than in others. Mountains, for example, are usually wetter than lowland areas.

Measuring rain

The amount of rain that falls is measured by the depth it fills a **rain gauge**. This is a special jar that collects rain. A very heavy rain storm can fill a rain gauge to a depth of 50 mm.

Convection rain

Rain showers usually fall from cumulus clouds. These clouds form as the ground warms up during the day and air containing water vapour rises. This type of heating is called **convection**. A rising 'bubble' of warm air is called a **thermal**.

The air cools down as it rises. This changes **water vapour** to tiny droplets of water. The droplets stay in the air because they are so light and because the air keeps rising under them. The droplets collide and grow as they move up and down in the cloud. When the droplets become too heavy to stay up, they fall as convection rain.

Mountain rain

Mountain ranges are some of the wettest places on Earth. This is because the air is forced up over them. As the air rises, it condenses to form cloud and rain.

Rain formed over mountains is called **relief rain**. Relief is a word used in geography to describe the shape of the land.

Hailstones

Some rain drops grow so big and become so cold that they fall as frozen drops of water called hailstones.

There are usually periods of sunshine in between the showers of rain and hail. In this type of weather, it is very hard to forecast exactly when or where it will rain, and if the sun will shine.

Hailstones are formed when freezing rising air makes rain drops grow and turn to ice.

The largest hailstones can measure several centimetres across.

Hailstones can flatten a field of crops and can even cause dents in cars.

Rain belts

It seems on some days as if it will never stop raining. At first, the rain falls as a light rain called drizzle. Then clouds become darker and lower. Rain becomes heavier and lasts for hour after hour. Then the sky suddenly clears again and the rain stops.

Rain on a front

A long period of rain that sweeps across a wide area is called a rain belt. Nowhere along the rain belt escapes the rain.

A rain belt is caused when an area of warm air slides up over colder air. As the warm air rises, it cools to form low stratus cloud.

The boundary line between the warm and the cold air is called a front.

Each area is called an **air mass**. A long period of rain can be expected as the front slowly moves forwards.

A change in pressure

One way to **forecast** when a rain belt is coming is to watch the air pressure on a **barometer**.

Air pressure is the weight of air that presses down on the ground. When air is rising, there is an area of low pressure. When it is sinking, there is high pressure.

People do not feel air pressure changes when they happen over several hours. When there is a quick change of pressure, you can sometimes feel a pop in your ears.

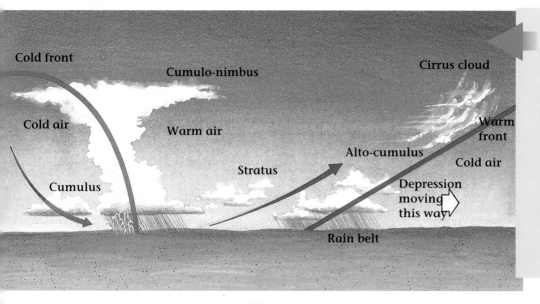

Cold front

Cumulo-nimbus

Cirrus cloud

Cold air

Warm air

Warm front

Cumulus

Alto-cumulus

Cold air

Stratus

Depression moving this way

Rain belt

A front divides two different types of air.

Warm air rises along a front and cools to form cloud and rain.

The front moves forward bringing a change in weather.

A satellite image that shows a depression moving across the UK.

Air spirals anticlockwise towards the centre of the depression.

The fronts can be seen as thick bands of cloud that stream out to the east towards Norway and to the south over France.

Depressions

Some areas of low pressure are also called **depressions**. Air spirals around a depression at the same time as it slowly rises.

In the northern hemisphere, the air spirals anticlockwise. In the southern hemisphere, it spirals clockwise. The wind becomes faster towards the centre of the depression.

Depressions that move over land from an ocean usually bring the most rain. They carry water that has been **evaporated** from the ocean.

Inside a depression, there is often a **warm front** where a band of warm air is moving towards an area of colder air. Rain falls along the area near the warm front.

There can also be a **cold front** where cold air is moving towards the warmer air. This gives more clouds and more rain.

Once the depression and its warm and cold fronts have passed, the sky becomes clearer again. Windy and bright weather with some showers can be expected to follow a depression.

Did you know?

Most depressions form and move in the middle latitudes. These are the areas between latitudes 30 and 60 degrees north and south.

Depressions usually move from west to east. They are blown by westerly winds in the middle latitudes.

Sometimes a cold front catches up with a warm front. This is called an *occluded front*.

Fog and frost

Fog in London on a cold winter night.

Some cars have special fog lights to beam through the fog.

Some types of weather bring special problems. Fog can stop people travelling and plays a part in causing accidents. Frost freezes water in the ground as well as water in pipes. Homes can be flooded when water leaks from pipes that have been burst by ice.

Conditions for fog

Fog is like cloud at ground level. It is made from billions of tiny water droplets. It forms when air with **water vapour** cools down. As it becomes colder, the water vapour starts to **condense** into tiny water droplets. Fog needs calm conditions to form. If the wind is blowing too fast, the air is blown away before it can settle and condense.

Autumn mists

Fog sometimes forms when warm, moist air moves over cold land. This often happens in the UK in autumn. Warm air from the south sometimes moves over land that is quickly cooling down.

On some nights, fog forms in valleys where the air is cold and damp. Drivers can have accidents if they drive too quickly into a **fog bank**. Dense fog banks form over the sea near Newfoundland in Canada. Air that has travelled over the warm Gulf Stream ocean current blows over the cold Labrador current. The warm moist air cools down and makes fog banks that can last for days.

Burnt off

Fog clears away when the sun warms up the air again. This changes the water droplets back to water vapour. Most fog is burnt off by midday. On very cold and calm days, the fog may not clear away at all.

Did you know?

Fog over many cities is made much worse when it mixes with exhaust fumes from cars and smoke from chimneys. This mixture of fog and smoke is called smog.

In proper fog, visibility is less than 1 km.

Dew and frost

On some mornings, the ground is wet with **dew**. This is because the air has become cold at night and water droplets have formed on grass and leaves.

Frost is created when the ground freezes hard and droplets of water in it change to ice. This often happens in winter when there is a clear sky at night. Without any cloud, heat from the day goes back into space. Clouds can bring rain, but also help keep the heat in at night.

Early morning mist over Glastonbury Tor in southwest England.

A weather forecast

There are many old sayings that try to **forecast** the weather. There are good reasons for some of them, but most are not very reliable.

A meteorologist's job

The job of studying the weather is done by **meteorologists**. They have to understand how the weather works so they can forecast what will happen next. To do this, they need figures about the **temperature**, rainfall, wind speed, air pressure and other weather elements. These figures are called data.

Getting data

Weather measurement data are recorded by weather stations on land and at sea. Weather balloons are sent up carrying instruments. Aircraft also give reports about the weather.

Weather satellites can see the weather all over the world. They measure the temperature of the air and sea. They also show where clouds are.

Most of the UK is now covered by radar stations that plot rain clouds and thunderstorms. In the USA, there are special **weather stations** to collect data about **hurricanes** and **tornadoes**.

From hundreds of kilometres above the Earth, a special satellite collects data about the weather. Some satellites circle the Earth in orbit. Others are fixed over one place.

Most weather data come from sensors that can detect differences in temperature. This data can be changed into maps and pictures.

Weather maps

Data about the weather are fed into computers to make weather maps. These are called **synoptic charts**. They help the meteorologists to forecast the weather. Most weather forecasts are accurate for a few days in advance, though sometimes there are mistakes.

Did you know?

Saint Swithun was a bishop of Winchester who died in 862. Saint Swithun's day is on July 15th. An old saying is that if it rains on Saint Swithun's day, it will rain for the next 40 days.

In 1870, the US Army set up an organization to forecast the weather. This became the US Weather Bureau.

Using the data

Weather data are needed by many different people. Farmers need to know when it is best to harvest their crops. Roads need to be gritted or covered with salt when icy weather is expected.

People in ships have to know what kind of weather to expect. They have their own **shipping forecast** because of their special safety needs. This divides the sea into different shipping areas. The waters around the UK are divided into zones with names such as Thames, Solent and Dogger.

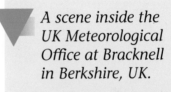

A scene inside the UK Meteorological Office at Bracknell in Berkshire, UK.

Computers are used to store and help make sense of all the weather data.

The water cycle

Water is always going somewhere. It moves as currents in the oceans. It flows in rivers and moves through the sky as **water vapour** or as clouds. It falls to the ground as rain and snow. Water moves from place to place in a set of links called the **water cycle**.

The cycle starts

The water cycle starts in the seas and oceans which contain salt water. The sun heats the top layer of water and **evaporates** it. This changes the water to water vapour. The salt is left behind.

Blown over land

The water vapour rises in the air, gradually cools down and some of it becomes clouds. Rain falls from some clouds back into the oceans.

Clouds are also blown by the wind over the land. More clouds form as air rises over warm ground and over mountains. Rain, hail and snow fall from these clouds. The word **precipitation** is used to describe all forms of water that fall to the ground.

A stream in the Pyrénées mountains between Spain and France.

Rain that falls on the mountains runs into streams and rivers.

The rivers flow back to the sea to complete the water cycle.

A downhill ride

Some rain falls on trees and other plants and is then evaporated back to the sky again. The rest runs off the surface or sinks through soil and rocks. This flows back to the sea in streams and rivers.

A few rivers flow down to lakes that are below sea level such as the Dead Sea. The water from these lakes slowly evaporates again.

An iceberg off the coast of Chile.

The ice has come from the Andes Mountains as a glacier.

The front of the glacier breaks off when it reaches the sea. The iceberg is melted by the warmer sea water.

Did you know?

The oceans contain 97% of the total water on Earth.

The amount of fresh water in lakes and rivers is only 0.01%, with 2% as ice.

In the USA, 4200 billion gallons of rain and snow fall each day on average. Of this, 1220 billion gallons flows back to the sea.

Glaciers and icebergs

Some water falls as snow and changes to ice. This slowly moves back to the sea as **glaciers**. Some glaciers never reach the sea. They melt long before they get there. Others reach the sea, break up and float away. This is how **icebergs** are formed.

The cycle completed

The water cycle is completed when water that started in the sea flows back to the sea. Then the cycle starts all over again.

Hurricane force

A storm hit southern England in 1987. Gusts of 120 mph blew down 15 million trees during one night. Roofs were ripped off buildings, walls were blown over and 19 people were killed. British people usually only read about this kind of weather happening in other countries.

Wind speed

The speed of the wind increases between a **gale**, a **storm** and a **hurricane**. A hurricane force wind starts at 120 kph and can go to over 300 kph. A hurricane is also known as a **cyclone**, **typhoon** or a **willi-willi** in different parts of the world.

Start of a hurricane

Hurricanes start to form over warm seas in tropical areas. The hot sun gives the energy to make the air rise quickly. The rising air begins to spin around the centre which is called the **eye**. Air pressure is very low because of the rising air.

Rising **water vapour** becomes tall, **dense** rain clouds. More air is sucked in from nearby areas of higher air pressure.

Most hurricanes start at the end of the hottest time of the year. There is a hurricane season for a few months until the sea and the air cool down again.

The circular swirl of cloud show two hurricanes.

These are both in the western part of the Pacific Ocean where they are called typhoons.

The typhoon on the left was named Odessa. The one on the right was named Pat.

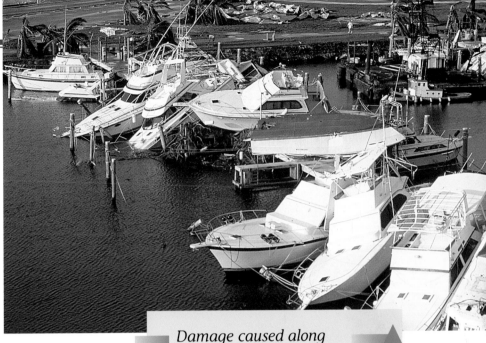

A hurricane strikes

A hurricane moves in a curving track that is hard to predict. Giant waves are blown onshore when it reaches land. Many people are drowned in places where there is no way to escape to higher ground. The winds are strong enough to blow out windows and to knock down all but the strongest buildings.

Far more damage is done in poor countries such as Bangladesh than in a richer country such as the USA. This is because the people in the USA can afford better warning systems and are able to build using stronger materials.

Hurricane names

Hurricanes are given boys' and girls' names. Hurricanes Erin and Felix struck the USA in 1995.

Hurricane Andrew hit Florida in 1992. It killed 65 people and caused millions of dollars worth of damage. The only way to survive a hurricane is to be ready, take shelter, or move out.

Damage caused along the coast when hurricane Andrew struck Florida in 1992.

The wind speed of this hurricane reached 320 kph.

Did you know?

Hurricanes are called cyclones in the Indian Ocean and typhoons in the Pacific Ocean. In Australia, they are called willi-willies.

In 1991, a cyclone killed 134,000 people on islands along the coast of Bangladesh. In 1994, another cyclone hit the same area and 300 people were killed. The difference is that in 1994, 800,000 people moved from the danger zone when the cyclone was *forecast*.

Drought

A **drought** is a long period without rain. Droughts can be a bigger problem in places where they are not expected, or in countries too poor to cope. This is because there are not enough supplies of water to last for long.

Causes of drought

Droughts in the UK are caused by weather conditions that bring warm and dry air. This can happen in summer when there is a high-pressure area called an **anticyclone**.

The dry months in Mali on the southern edge of the Sahara desert.

Dry sand and scattered trees show the effects of a drought.

Air in an anticyclone slowly sinks and spins out. It becomes warmer as it sinks. This is the opposite to the conditions needed for rain. Warm air can hold more **water vapour** than cold air. So even if there is water vapour in the air, it is not likely that it will rain.

Rains that fail

There have been several droughts in Africa in recent years. Since 1989, there have been droughts in Ethiopia, Mali, Sudan and other countries close to the Sahara desert. These are countries where there is usually a dry season with no rain. This is then followed by a rainy season when it is hot and **cumulus** clouds form. Sometimes the rain clouds do not form. The conditions are not always right. It is very hard to predict when this will happen.

The effects of drought

A drought can ruin a farmer's crops. This is a special problem in countries where most farmers and their families eat the food they grow. They do not have enough money to buy food from other countries.

Rivers dry up and there is no water for either people or animals. If the supply of food runs out, there can be a **famine**. This is when food aid is needed.

In richer countries, reservoirs hold back enough water for dry periods, though it has to be used carefully.

Causing problems

Drought has been made worse in countries where too many trees have been cut down. There is no shade without trees so the ground is baked even harder. Soil becomes infertile because there is no rotting vegetation. Any rain that does fall washes away the unprotected soil.

Dry and cracked ground on the bed of a lake in Australia.

In 1994, the Murray-Darling river stopped flowing during one of Australia's worst recent droughts. This is the world's fourteenth largest river.

Did you know?

Dust from the Sahara desert sometimes falls on the UK. It is blown north in an *anticyclone*.

Scientists can see how crops are growing in any part of the world using *weather satellites*. They know if there will be a famine long before it happens.

Thunder and lightning

A bright streak of lightning followed by a loud clap or rumble of **thunder** can be terrifying. Nobody is safe either indoors or in the open. Luckily, the chances of being hit are very small. In the UK, about five people are killed every year by lightning.

Electric sparks

Lightning is a giant electric spark. Electricity builds up in giant cumulo-nimbus clouds. This may be caused by large raindrops and hailstones as they move up then fall back down in the cloud. A positive electric charge builds up. The electrical energy is suddenly released when the spark jumps to somewhere with a negative charge. This can be the ground or another part of the cloud.

Different shapes

There are different types of lightning. **Sheet lightning** makes the whole cloud glow white for a second. **Forked lightning** splits up on its way to the ground. The white streak is caused by the great heat that passes through the air. The temperature of the air reaches 27760°C.

Forked lightning streaks to the ground during a storm in Tuscon, Arizona, USA.

Damage to a telegraph pole caused by a lightning strike. The tall pole and metal wires attracted the lightning.

There are about 300,000 lightning ground strikes in the UK every year.

The sound of thunder

Thunder is the sound made when air is heated by lightning and expands. There is a sudden crack of sound if the lightning is nearly overhead, or a low rumble if it is far away.

Lightning can always be seen before the thunder is heard. This is because light travels faster than sound. The sound takes about 3 seconds to travel 1 km.

First strike

Lightning often strikes trees and tall buildings. These are the first things it meets on the way to the ground. However, a metal object as small as a bracelet can attract a streak of lightning. Lightning is often the cause of fires in forests and grasslands in Australia and Africa.

Keep safe

One way to stop damage is to have a **lightning conductor**. This is a metal strip from the top of a building to the ground. This gives a safe path for the electricity to follow. If caught in the open, the safest thing to do is to crouch down on the ground.

Did you know?

In 1995, a woman in Nottingham was struck by lightning when she opened her fridge door. The lightning had hit the house and run through the electrical wires.

An instrument used to record lightning is called a brontometer.

In 1923, during one storm over London that lasted 6 hours, 6924 separate lighting flashes were recorded.

Snow and ice

A covering of snow completely changes a landscape. It makes it attractive to look at and fun to play in, but it can also be very dangerous.

Crystals of ice

Snow is one way that water comes to the ground. Snow forms in a cloud when there are freezing **temperatures**. **Water vapour** is changed into small crystals of ice instead of into drops of water. The crystals join with others until a snowflake is formed. One snowflake can be made from several hundred ice crystals.

Snowflakes

The size of a snowflake depends on the temperature. The largest flakes fall when the temperature is just below freezing point at 0°C. The smallest flakes fall when the temperature is even colder.

The larger flakes often melt as they fall through the sky or as soon as they reach the ground. If the snow is melting as it falls, it turns to a form of rain called sleet. Thick snow driven by strong wind causes a blizzard.

A winter scene in New York, USA.

The snow is about 1 metre thick which is about the same amount of water as 10 cm of rain.

Snow like this is very heavy to shovel. Every year, doctors warn people of the danger of heart attacks brought on by clearing snow from paths and drives.

A Canadian Coast Guard ice breaker smashes a way through ice to clear a path for another ship.

Icy lakes

Water turns to ice when the temperature falls below freezing point. A layer of ice forms on the surface of lakes and rivers. Even the sea can change to ice and freeze in the shape of waves. Special ships called **ice breakers** are needed to force their way through sea pack ice.

The snow line

There is always snow above the snow line on the world's highest mountains. As snow gets thicker, the weight presses down on layers of snow beneath. This changes the lower layers to ice. This is how a **glacier** starts.

Snow depth

Snow that settles can quickly become deeper. The depth of snow is about ten times the depth that would have fallen if it had rained. This means that the water from 1 cm of rain would give 10 cm depth of snow.

Once snow settles, the wind can blow it into deep piles called snow drifts. These pile up in hollows and against hedges and walls.

Funnels of destruction

In March 1994, a **tornado** hit a church in Alabama where 150 people were at prayer. The roof was ripped off and walls collapsed. Seventeen people were killed. The rest were lucky to survive. This was one of about 150 tornadoes that cut a deadly path through the USA that year. The central states are a part of the world where tornadoes can be expected. This is why they are known as 'tornado alley'.

Tornado strength

A tornado is one of nature's most violent weather forces. Air spins around in a narrow funnel at a speed of up to 700 kph. Tornadoes are also known as 'twisters' because of the way they curve from the clouds to the ground, spinning and twisting.

Inside a tornado

Tornadoes are usually no wider than 500 metres. They stretch from the ground to the base of thunder clouds. They are centres of extreme low pressure with a narrow **eye** in the middle. The strong winds rotate around and up the sides of the eye.

A tornado moves over the ground in a way that is impossible to predict. Sometimes they are above ground level, then suddenly they snake down all the way. Their path can be followed by looking for the destruction they leave behind.

Where and when

Tornadoes form over land along a front where hot moist air meets cold dry air. This happens mainly in spring and early summer.

A tornado spirals from dark rain clouds to the ground over the plains of North America.

The tornado sucks up soil to make it black.

It is impossible to predict exactly where this twister will go next.

Damage to buildings in Illinois, USA, after a tornado struck the area.

It is too expensive to build houses strong enough to survive a direct hit from a tornado.

People depend on weather forecasters to warn them when a tornado is likely to come.

There are also tornadoes in the UK. These are not as common or as powerful as in the USA.

Into the cellar

It is very hard to build anything strong enough to survive a tornado. The strength of the wind causes most of the damage.

It is possible for buildings to explode in the area near a tornado. Air at high pressure in a building pushes outwards towards the low pressure created by the tornado, so the building explodes. Most homes in 'tornado alley' have been built with a cellar. Nowhere else is safe.

A waterspout

A **waterspout** is like a tornado but it forms over the sea. The force of the wind can suck water, fish and even small boats up into the air.

In 1994, fish suddenly appeared on the ground in Northern Territory, Australia. One explanation was that they were sucked up by a tornado then dropped when it rained.

Did you know?

A tornado can travel over the land at about 90 kph.

One theory about the circular shape and the reason for the ancient stones at Stonehenge is that they are a reminder of a tornado that hit the area in prehistoric times.

Mediterranean climate

Europe is separated from Africa by the Mediterranean Sea. Countries around the Mediterranean Sea such as Spain, Greece and Italy are some of the world's most popular holiday areas. Other countries such as Turkey and Tunisia are also becoming popular. The sea and the Mediterranean climate are two of the main reasons for this.

Early summer on the Spanish holiday island of Ibiza.

The holiday homes are close together for shade and painted white to reflect the heat. Small windows also keep them cool inside.

Summer sun

Places that have a Mediterranean climate have hot summer months when the average **temperature** for the day is about 25°C. During the middle of the day, the temperature can go as high as 40°C. Tourists can be fairly sure that it will not rain much, at least from the start of June to the end of August.

This is especially a problem for people from colder countries such as the UK and Sweden who may have fair, sensitive skin.

Take care

There are some **thunderstorms** but these are rare. For tourists, the main problem is how to enjoy the sun and stop sunburn at the same time. Burnt skin can cause skin cancer.

Rain in winter

During the winter, rain belts sweep in from the Atlantic Ocean. The temperature drops, though the average for the coldest month does not usually go below 10°C.

The climate explained

There are several other places around the world that also have a Mediterranean climate. For example, California and southern parts of Australia have the same high summer temperatures and mild, wet winters.

Places with a Mediterranean climate have two things in common. They are all at about latitude 35 degrees north or south of the equator. This position means that the sun is high in the sky during the summer, though it is never vertically overhead. A high angle of the sun means high temperatures.

They are also on the western side of a continent. This allows depressions to move in from an ocean during the winter bringing rain.

Life in the sun

People who live in a Mediterranean climate often stay out of the midday summer sun. Work stops until it is cooler.

In the USA, the Mediterranean climate has attracted people and businesses to California. It is a climate that people can enjoy, as long as they are able to get water during the summer drought.

Did you know?

The sunny weather was one reason why so many films used to be made in California at Hollywood. This made it easier to film out of doors all year round.

In some Australian schools children are not allowed to play outside unless they are wearing a hat to protect them from the sun.

A winter scene in Venice, Italy.

Men are standing in the street, well prepared for the rain and the winter temperatures.

Hot desert climates

There are some places where very few people live because it is too dry. These places are called **deserts**. It is no wonder that these places are so deserted.

Lack of rain

A hot desert is a place where there is very little rain and where the **temperature** is high all year. Areas with less than 250 mm of rain in a year are called deserts.

Hot desert sun

Hot deserts are directly under the tropics. The Sahara desert is directly under the Tropic of Cancer at latitude 23½ degrees north.

The Great Australian Desert is under the Tropic of Capricorn at 23½ degrees south.

The sun is directly over the Tropic of Cancer at 12 noon for one day of the year on June 22nd. This makes the daytime summer temperature very hot. Even when the sun is directly over the Tropic of Capricorn, the angle of the sun is still high over the tropic of Cancer. The night-time temperature is very much colder. This is because there is no cloud to keep in the day's heat.

A hot desert area in Death Valley, California, USA.

Pieces of rock are broken off and become sand as the rock is weakened by heating during the day, then cooling at night.

Mauretania is a country in North Africa that is mostly in the Sahara desert.

Strong winds blow the sand over roads and sometimes over villages and towns.

Fences are being planted to stop the sand from moving.

Sinking air

The hot deserts are so dry because the air over them is usually sinking. As the air sinks, it warms up so clouds do not form and there is no rain.

Life in the desert

In the past, few people were able to survive in a desert. Now, water can be brought through pipes and canals to places that are dry. It can also be extracted from rocks deep underground. The air can be kept cool by air conditioning. All this is expensive but it is a price that many people are willing to pay.

Did you know?

In August 1994, the temperature in Death Valley, California, reached 52°C. The record for the area is 53°C. This makes it one of the hottest places on Earth.

Some desert countries are rich because they have oil to sell. Saudi Arabia and Kuwait in the Middle East are two examples.

It does sometimes rain in a desert. Then there can be flash floods that rush down dried-up valleys.

There are also cold deserts such as in Antarctica. The precipitation is below 250 mm but the temperatures can be freezing.

The British climate

People say that the UK does not have a climate. It only has weather! This is because there are so many changes in rain, wind, clouds and sun from day to day.

British summer

The UK is between latitude 50 and 60 degrees north of the equator. The sun is never directly overhead at this latitude. Its highest angle in June is 60 degrees. The summer is usually warm at about 18°C, but this can vary from day to day. There are up to 16 hours of daylight at the height of the summer.

Winter time

The sun is at its lowest angle in winter. Even at noon, it is very low in the sky, at only about 12 degrees. The **temperature** is only a few degrees above freezing point. There are less than 10 hours of daylight in mid-winter.

Isotherms

The temperature is shown on a map by drawing lines called **isotherms**. These show that the northern areas of the British Isles are colder in the summer than in the south. In winter, the eastern side is colder than the west.

A fine summer day in Southport near Liverpool, UK.

*There is a bright blue sky with some scattered **cumulus** cloud.*

A winter landscape on an upland area in England.

Snow has fallen on the hills. It stays longer on the hills because the temperature is lower where the land is higher.

Did you know?

The west coast of North America in Washington, USA, and British Columbia in Canada have a similar type of climate to the UK.

There is nowhere in the UK where snow stays permanently on the ground. Even on Ben Nevis at 1344 metres, the winter snow melts by early summer.

When the wind blows

The Atlantic ocean is to the west of the British Isles. The wind blows mostly from the west throughout the year. This brings rain in every month. Much of the rain comes from **depressions** that move across the UK from west to east.

Winds sometimes blow from the east and the north in winter. This brings very cold air over the country, sometimes causing snowfalls.

The hottest air blows from the south. This comes from either tropical parts of the Atlantic Ocean or from the Sahara desert.

North Atlantic Drift

A warm ocean current called the **North Atlantic Drift** is continually flowing across the Atlantic Ocean from west to east. This brings warm water towards the UK. This is one reason why the sea does not freeze in winter and why winter temperatures are mild.

The wet tropics

Tropical climates are the wettest and the hottest types of climate on Earth. This is the area between the Tropic of Cancer at latitude 23½ degrees north and the Tropic of Capricorn at 23½ degrees south.

Along the equator

The equator is half way between the two tropics. Near to the equator, the **temperature** does not change much from day to day. It is hot all year round, usually at about 30°C. This is because the angle of the sun is always high in the sky at midday.

The sun is directly overhead on two days of the year. This is when the tilt of the Earth seems to move the sun from the northern hemisphere to the southern hemisphere across the line of the equator at 0 degree latitude.

Daily rain

The high temperatures mean that there is a large amount of **evaporation**. Hot, moist air rises from early morning. By the afternoon, it has cooled down to become dark thunderclouds. These give heavy rain showers.

Rainwater is collected on the surfaces of leaves where there is a rain forest. The next day, there is more evaporation so the weather is the same again.

The savannah

Further from the equator, the tropical climate becomes more seasonal. There are two main seasons. One season is warm and very dry. The other is hot and can be wet. This type of climate is called a **savannah climate**.

Macaws in the rain forest in Brazil.

The average daily temperature at Belem, 1 degree south, in Brazil ranges from 26.1°C in the coldest month to 26.9°C in the hottest month.

Savannah rains

Most rain comes from **cumulus** clouds that build up because of the heat. This rain is very unreliable. In some years, there is too much and in other years, there is almost none. Some of the worst **famines** have been in places with a savannah climate such as the African countries of Chad and Sudan.

The monsoon winds

The **monsoon climates** are where the winds blow from the land for one part of the year. This brings very dry weather.

They then blow from the ocean for the rest of the year. This brings wet weather. India and other countries in South-East Asia have this type of climate. It is very hard for farmers to cope with so much rain at one time of year, then none at all for the rest.

Did you know?

The hours of daylight and darkness in one 24 hour period are exactly the same all year round along the equator.

The Tropic of Cancer and the Tropic of Capricorn are the furthest places north and south of the equator where the sun is ever directly overhead. This happens at 12 noon for one day at each place.

A heavy downpour during the monsoon rains in Bangladesh.

The wind blows from the Indian Ocean bringing heavy rain for about 4 months.

The remainder of the year has very little rain.

The changing climate

Some scientists believe that the Earth's climates have started to change. There have been changes to climates in the past, for example, during the Ice Age. This time, people are causing the changes.

The carbon cycle

Different gases make up the Earth's **atmosphere**. Some, such as carbon dioxide, are taken into plants and into the soil. Plants use it to grow leaves and branches. They breathe out oxygen. When a plant dies, the carbon dioxide is released into the air again.

Some rocks, such as coal, are the fossilized remains of plants. These hold the carbon until the coal is worn away by the weather or burnt. There is also carbon in oil.

The problem is that a very large amount of oil and coal is burnt to generate electricity and to power vehicles. This is putting far more carbon dioxide into the air than happens naturally.

Global warming

Carbon dioxide lets heat come through the atmosphere from the sun. Heat reflected back from the ground is trapped by the carbon dioxide. This may be causing the Earth's atmosphere to become warmer. This is known as **global warming**.

Burning trees in the Amazon rain forest.

About one third of all carbon in the world's vegetation is in the tropical rain forests.

Global warming could make the Earth's average **temperatures** one or more degrees higher over the next 100 years. This does not sound much but the effects could be serious.

Warmer temperatures mean that there could be more violent storms, heavier rain or long periods of drought. Buildings will have to be made stronger and more reservoirs will be needed.

Rising seas

One of the greatest dangers from global warming is that the seas and oceans will rise. Water expands when it is heated and there will also be more melted ice from glaciers and ice sheets.

Low-lying islands and lowlands all over the world are the first places at risk. Higher sea levels mean more flooding. It will be very expensive to guard against this.

Did you know?

In 1995, an iceberg the size of Oxfordshire broke away from the Antarctic ice shelf. This might be an early sign of global warming.

In 1995, there was about twice as much carbon dioxide in the atmosphere as there was in 1895.

EDUCATIONAL
RESOURCE SERVICE

Glossary

air mass a body of air with its own temperature and moisture

anticyclone an area of high pressure with sinking air that circles around it

aspect the direction a slope faces

atmosphere the layer of gases around the Earth

barometer an instrument used to measure air pressure

Beaufort scale a scale used to measure wind strength

cirrus cloud at very high level

cold front a line with warm air in front and colder air moving forward

condensation a gas changed to a liquid

convection the process where air that is heated rises

cumulus a type of cloud with a fluffy appearance

current a flow of water across an ocean

cyclone the name for a hurricane in the Indian Ocean

depression an area of low pressure with winds that circle and rise

desert an area where there is less than 250 mm of rain each year

dew droplets of water that form on surfaces near the ground

drought a long period with no rain

equinoxes times of the year when there are equal hours of day and night

evaporate to change from a liquid to a gas by heating

eye the calm centre of a hurricane

famine a time where there is a severe shortage of food

fog bank a large area of fog

forecast a prediction about the weather

forked lightning lightning that branches in different directions

gale a wind speed of 62–74 kph

glacier a very slow moving mass of ice in a mountain valley

global warming a theory that says the temperature of the Earth's atmosphere is becoming warmer

hemisphere a half of the Earth

hurricane an area of intense low pressure with wind speeds over 119 kph

ice breaker a ship used to break through ice

isotherms lines on a weather map that link together places with the same temperature

lightning conductor a strip of metal used to bring lightning safely to the ground

meteorologist a person whose job is to study and forecast the weather

monsoon a seasonal change in the wind direction

monsoon climate a climate that has a seasonal change in wind direction

North Atlantic Drift a warm ocean current in the North Atlantic ocean

occluded front a front where the warm and cold fronts have joined at ground level

precipitation all forms of water that fall to the ground, such as rain and snow

prevailing winds winds that mainly blow from one direction

radiation heat and light energy from the sun or other sources

rain gauge an instrument used to measure rainfall

relief rain rain that forms and falls over mountains

savannah climate a type of tropical climate which has seasonal changes in rainfall

sheet lightning lightning that makes a cloud glow white

shipping forecast a prediction about the weather at sea

storm (force) wind speeds of 82–102 kph

stratus a layer of cloud

summer solstice the time when the sun is highest in the sky and daylight hours longest

synoptic charts maps with weather data

temperature the amount of heat

temperature inversion a temperature that is colder at lower levels and warmer higher up

thermal a rising 'bubble' of warm air

thermometer an instrument used to measure temperature

thunder a loud noise made when air is heated by lightning

thunderstorm short period with heavy rain, thunder and lightning and gusting winds

tornado a funnel of air rotating at very high speed

trade winds winds that blow towards the equator from the tropics

troposphere the lowest layer of the atmosphere

typhoon the name for a hurricane in the Indian Ocean

warm front a line with cold air in front and warmer air moving forward

water cycle the movement of water from the oceans to the land then back again

water vapour water in the form of a gas

waterspout a funnel of air rotating at very high speed over water that draws spray up into it

weather satellites a space satellite used to collect data about the weather

weather stations a place where weather instruments record the weather

willi-willi the name for a hurricane in the Java Sea

Index

Numbers in plain type (6) refer to the text. Numbers in italic type (*11*) refer to a caption.